Copyright © 2023 by M.J. Knightly (Author)

This book is protected by copyright law and is intended solely for personal use. Reproduction, distribution, or any other form of use requires the written permission of the author. The information presented in this book is for educational and entertainment purposes only, and while every effort has been made to ensure its accuracy and completeness, no guarantees are made. The author is not providing legal, financial, medical, or professional advice, and readers should consult with a licensed professional before implementing any of the techniques discussed in this book. The content in this book has been sourced from various reliable sources, but readers should exercise their own judgment when using this information. The author is not responsible for any losses, direct or indirect, that may occur from the use of this book, including but not limited to errors, omissions, or inaccuracies.

We hope this book has been informative and helpful on your journey to understanding and celebrating older adults. Thank you for your interest and support!

Title: Evolution of Transportation: From Hooves to Wheels

Subtitle: Domestication and Early Vehicles

Series: Ride Through Time: The Story of World Vehicles

By M.J. Knightly

"The transportation industry is on the brink of a revolution, with advancements in autonomous vehicles, electric cars, and new modes of transportation like hyperloops and vertical takeoff and landing aircrafts."
Mary Barra, CEO of General Motors

"Innovation in transportation is not only about speed and efficiency, but also about sustainability and reducing our impact on the environment."
Patricia Espinosa, Executive Secretary of the United Nations Framework Convention on Climate Change

"The future of transportation will be about creating a seamless and integrated experience, where different modes of transportation work together to get people where they need to go."
Dara Khosrowshahi, CEO of Uber

"The age of electric vehicles is here, and it's exciting to see how technology is driving the transformation of our transportation systems."
Elon Musk, CEO of Tesla and SpaceX

"Transportation is not just about getting from point A to point B, it's about the freedom and opportunities that come with mobility. Innovations in transportation are critical for empowering individuals and communities around the world."
Ban Ki-moon, former Secretary-General of the United Nations

"As transportation continues to evolve, we have the opportunity to create a more equitable and accessible system that benefits all people, regardless of their background or circumstances."
Keisha Lance Bottoms, former mayor of Atlanta, Georgia

"Innovation is key to unlocking the potential of transportation, and we need to encourage and invest in new ideas and technologies that will shape the future of mobility."
Hiroto Saikawa, former CEO of Nissan Motor Company

Table of Contents

Introduction 9
The Evolution of Transportation: A Brief Overview 9
Animal-Drawn Transportation: A Historical Perspective 12
The Importance of Animal-Drawn Transportation in Human History 15

Chapter 1: The Early Days of Animal-Drawn Transportation 18
Prehistoric Transport: Using Animals for Hunting and Travel 18
The Emergence of Domesticated Animals for Transportation 20
The Development of Wheeled Vehicles for Animal-Drawn Transportation 23
The Advantages and Limitations of Animal-Drawn Transportation 26

Chapter 2: Animal-Drawn Transportation in the Ancient World 29
Animal-Drawn Transportation in Mesopotamia and Egypt 29
The Use of Chariots in Ancient Greece and Rome 32
The Role of Camels and Horses in the Silk Road Trade .. 35

The Decline of Animal-Drawn Transportation in the Middle Ages 38

Chapter 3: The Renaissance of Animal-Drawn Transportation 41

The Rediscovery of Classical Learning and Culture 41

The Renaissance of Art, Science, and Technology 44

The Role of Animal-Drawn Transportation in Renaissance Society 47

The Evolution of Carriages and Coaches 50

Chapter 4: The Age of Horse-Drawn Transportation 53

The Industrial Revolution and the Rise of the Horse-Drawn Carriage 53

The Importance of Horses in Agriculture and Trade 57

The Advent of Streetcars and Omnibuses 60

The Impact of Horse-Drawn Transportation on Urbanization 63

Chapter 5: The Limits of Animal-Drawn Transportation 66

The Environmental and Social Costs of Animal-Drawn Transportation 66

The Health and Welfare of Animals Used in Transportation 69

The Challenges of Maintenance, Fuel, and Speed 72

    The Rise of Competition from Steam and Internal Combustion Engines 75

Chapter 6: The Legacy of Animal-Drawn Transportation 78
    The Enduring Symbolism of Horse-Drawn Carriages ... 78
    The Preservation and Restoration of Antique Carriages 80
    The Continued Use of Animals for Transportation in Developing Countries 83
    The Lessons of Animal-Drawn Transportation for Modern Mobility 86

Chapter 7: The Future of Animal-Drawn Transportation 90
    The Emergence of Sustainable and Ethical Animal-Drawn Transportation 90
    The Use of Animal-Drawn Transportation in Tourism and Recreation 94
    The Prospects for Combining Animal-Drawn Transportation with Modern Technology 97
    The Potential of Animal-Drawn Transportation for a More Sustainable and Equitable World 100

Conclusion 104
    The Significance of Animal-Drawn Transportation in Human History 104

The Importance of Learning from the Past in Shaping the Future *108*
The Implications of Animal-Drawn Transportation for Contemporary Mobility *111*
Key Terms and Definitions **114**
Supporting Materials **116**

Introduction

The Evolution of Transportation: A Brief Overview

Transportation has played a significant role in human history, allowing people to travel farther, faster, and more efficiently than ever before. From early humans taming animals for transportation to the invention of the wheel and the development of modern cars and airplanes, transportation has undergone a remarkable evolution over the centuries. In this chapter, we will provide a brief overview of this evolution, highlighting the major milestones and innovations that have shaped transportation as we know it today.

The chapter will begin with an exploration of prehistoric transportation, discussing how early humans used animals for hunting and travel. We will then delve into the emergence of domesticated animals for transportation and the development of wheeled vehicles, which allowed humans to transport goods and people over greater distances. We will also examine the advantages and limitations of animal-drawn transportation, including its impact on agriculture, trade, and urbanization.

Moving on to the ancient world, we will explore the use of animal-drawn transportation in Mesopotamia, Egypt, Greece, and Rome, highlighting the role of chariots and other vehicles in warfare, commerce, and leisure. We will also discuss the importance of camels and horses in the Silk Road trade, which facilitated cultural and economic exchange between Asia and Europe.

Next, we will examine the Renaissance period, during which the rediscovery of classical learning and culture led to a renewed interest in art, science, and technology. We will discuss how animal-drawn transportation played a vital role in Renaissance society, including the evolution of carriages and coaches, which became symbols of luxury and social status.

Moving on to the Industrial Revolution, we will explore how the rise of steam power and internal combustion engines transformed transportation, leading to the advent of trains, automobiles, and airplanes. We will also discuss the environmental and social costs of these developments, including the impact of fossil fuels on climate change and the displacement of workers in traditional transportation industries.

Finally, we will examine the future of transportation, including the emergence of sustainable and ethical animal-drawn transportation, the use of animal-drawn transportation in tourism and recreation, and the prospects for combining animal-drawn transportation with modern technology. We will also discuss the potential of animal-drawn transportation for creating a more sustainable and equitable world.

Overall, this chapter will provide readers with a broad understanding of the evolution of transportation, setting the stage for the more detailed explorations of animal-drawn transportation throughout history that will follow in subsequent chapters.

Animal-Drawn Transportation: A Historical Perspective

Animal-drawn transportation has a rich history that spans thousands of years, and has played a crucial role in shaping human societies throughout the ages. From the early days of domestication to the modern use of animals in transportation, the use of animals as a means of transportation has been integral to human development and progress.

The historical perspective of animal-drawn transportation can be traced back to the prehistoric era, where early humans used animals for hunting and travel. The use of horses, camels, and oxen for transportation dates back to ancient civilizations such as Mesopotamia, Egypt, Greece, and Rome, where animal-drawn transportation was widely used for trade and warfare.

Animal-drawn transportation continued to be a significant aspect of daily life during the Renaissance era, where it played a crucial role in transportation for the wealthy and royal families. The era also saw the rise of carriages and coaches, which were used for transportation and social status.

During the Industrial Revolution, the role of animal-drawn transportation changed significantly, as horses became a vital part of agriculture and trade. The development of streetcars and omnibuses also transformed urban transportation, which in turn led to the growth of cities and urbanization.

While animal-drawn transportation has had many advantages, there have also been challenges associated with it. The environmental and social costs of animal-drawn transportation, as well as the health and welfare of animals, have been a significant concern. The emergence of competition from steam and internal combustion engines also challenged the use of animal-drawn transportation, leading to its decline in many parts of the world.

Despite these challenges, animal-drawn transportation continues to have an enduring legacy. In some parts of the world, animals are still used for transportation due to their accessibility and affordability, particularly in developing countries. The preservation and restoration of antique carriages have also become a popular hobby, with many enthusiasts working to maintain the legacy of animal-drawn transportation.

As we move towards a more sustainable future, the potential of animal-drawn transportation cannot be ignored. Sustainable and ethical animal-drawn transportation can offer an environmentally friendly alternative to modern transportation methods, and can play a crucial role in creating a more sustainable and equitable world.

In this book, we will explore the evolution of animal-drawn transportation, from the early days of domestication to its impact on human societies throughout history. We will examine the challenges and advantages associated with animal-drawn transportation, and the potential for animal-drawn transportation to play a role in the future of sustainable mobility.

The Importance of Animal-Drawn Transportation in Human History

The use of animal-drawn transportation has been a fundamental aspect of human history for thousands of years. From the earliest civilizations to the modern era, animals have played a significant role in transporting people and goods. This chapter will explore the importance of animal-drawn transportation throughout history.

One of the most significant contributions of animal-drawn transportation is the way it facilitated trade and commerce. In the early days of human history, animals such as horses, oxen, and camels were used to transport goods over long distances, opening up new markets and creating economic opportunities. Animal-drawn transportation also made it possible to transport heavy loads that would have been impossible to move otherwise. For example, in ancient Egypt, donkeys were used to transport building materials such as limestone blocks for the construction of the pyramids.

Animal-drawn transportation also played a crucial role in the movement of people. Before the invention of cars, trains, and airplanes, horses, donkeys, and camels were the primary mode of transportation for long distances. Whether for trade, migration, or warfare, animals provided a means for humans to travel great distances quickly and efficiently.

In addition to facilitating trade and travel, animal-drawn transportation also had a significant impact on social organization and culture. In many societies, owning horses or other valuable animals was a sign of wealth and prestige, and the use of animal-drawn vehicles was often reserved for the wealthy and powerful. The use of animal-drawn vehicles in parades and processions was also an important cultural tradition in many societies.

Animal-drawn transportation has also had a profound impact on the environment. The use of animals for transportation has allowed humans to access and exploit natural resources that would have been otherwise inaccessible. For example, the use of horses and mules allowed miners to transport ore and other materials from remote locations, enabling the development of mining industries that were critical to the economic development of many regions.

However, the use of animal-drawn transportation has not been without its problems. One of the most significant issues has been the welfare of the animals themselves. The use of animals for transportation can be physically demanding and sometimes cruel, and throughout history, many animals have suffered as a result of their use in transportation. The environmental impact of animal-drawn transportation has also been significant, with the overgrazing of pasturelands and the pollution of water sources being just two examples of the negative effects.

Despite its challenges, the importance of animal-drawn transportation in human history cannot be overstated. It has played a critical role in the development of trade, travel, and culture, and has allowed humans to access and exploit natural resources in ways that would have been impossible without the assistance of animals. Understanding the historical significance of animal-drawn transportation is essential for appreciating its place in contemporary society and for shaping the future of mobility.

Chapter 1: The Early Days of Animal-Drawn Transportation

Prehistoric Transport: Using Animals for Hunting and Travel

The use of animals for transportation has a long history, stretching back to prehistoric times. For early humans, the ability to travel quickly and efficiently was crucial for survival. While they did not have access to wheeled vehicles or harnesses, they did have a variety of animals at their disposal that they could use for hunting and travel.

One of the earliest and most common uses of animals for transportation was for hunting. Early humans would use dogs to track and chase prey, helping them to hunt more efficiently. In addition to dogs, other animals such as wolves, hyenas, and even bears were used for hunting in different regions of the world.

As humans began to settle in one place and establish communities, they also started using animals for transportation beyond just hunting. One of the earliest examples of this was the domestication of the donkey in Africa around 4000 BCE. Donkeys were well-suited for the arid conditions of the desert and could carry heavy loads long distances, making them valuable for trade and transportation.

In other regions of the world, different animals were domesticated and used for transportation. In Asia, for example, the horse was domesticated around 4000 BCE and quickly became an important mode of transportation, both for travel and for military purposes. In the Americas, llamas and alpacas were domesticated and used by the Incas for transportation in the Andes Mountains.

Despite the benefits of using animals for transportation, there were also limitations. Animals could only carry so much weight, and they required food and water, making long journeys difficult. In addition, using animals for transportation was not always safe, as they could be unpredictable and pose a danger to their handlers.

Despite these challenges, the use of animals for transportation continued to evolve over time. As humans developed new tools and technologies, they were able to harness animals more effectively and create more efficient modes of transportation. This eventually led to the development of wheeled vehicles, which allowed humans to transport goods and people more quickly and efficiently than ever before.

The Emergence of Domesticated Animals for Transportation

As human societies grew and developed, so too did their reliance on animal power for transportation. The domestication of animals allowed for greater efficiency and reliability in moving people and goods over long distances, and was a key development in the history of transportation.

Domestication of Animals

The domestication of animals for transportation likely began around 4000 BCE, when horses and donkeys were first domesticated in the Eurasian steppes. These animals were ideal for transportation due to their strength, endurance, and ability to travel over rough terrain. Other animals that were domesticated for transportation include oxen, camels, elephants, reindeer, and llamas.

The domestication of animals allowed for the development of specialized breeds that were better suited for transportation tasks, such as the heavy draft horses used for plowing and hauling in agriculture, or the swift Arabian horses bred for riding and racing. The use of domesticated animals also allowed for greater control over breeding and genetics, enabling humans to selectively breed animals for desired traits such as size, strength, and speed.

Animal-Drawn Transportation

The earliest forms of animal-drawn transportation were likely simple sleds or travois pulled by dogs or reindeer, used by hunter-gatherer societies to transport their belongings as they migrated across the land. As agricultural societies emerged, the use of draft animals such as oxen and horses became more common for plowing fields and hauling crops to market.

In addition to agriculture, animal-drawn transportation was also used for trade and commerce, allowing goods to be transported over long distances with greater efficiency and speed. The Silk Road, a network of trade routes that connected China with the Mediterranean world, relied heavily on the use of camels and horses for transportation.

Impact on Human Society

The emergence of domesticated animals for transportation had a significant impact on human society. It allowed for the development of larger and more complex societies by facilitating trade and commerce, enabling the growth of cities and the establishment of empires. Animal-drawn transportation also played a crucial role in warfare, allowing armies to travel quickly and transport supplies to the front lines.

However, the use of animals for transportation also had its drawbacks. It required significant resources to feed and maintain the animals, and could lead to overgrazing and environmental degradation in areas where large numbers of animals were kept. The use of animals for transportation also required significant expertise and skill, and accidents or injuries could be common.

Conclusion

The emergence of domesticated animals for transportation was a key development in the history of transportation, allowing for greater efficiency and reliability in moving people and goods over long distances. It had a significant impact on human society, enabling the growth of cities and the establishment of empires, and playing a crucial role in warfare and trade. However, the use of animals for transportation also had its drawbacks, requiring significant resources and expertise, and contributing to environmental degradation in some areas.

The Development of Wheeled Vehicles for Animal-Drawn Transportation

The use of animals for transportation was a significant step forward in the history of human mobility, but it was the development of wheeled vehicles that truly revolutionized transportation. Wheeled vehicles offered a number of advantages over animal-drawn sledges and travois, including greater speed, efficiency, and comfort.

The earliest wheeled vehicles were simple carts and wagons, which were used to transport goods and people over short distances. These vehicles were often made from local materials such as wood and animal hides, and were drawn by oxen, donkeys, or other domesticated animals. While the first wheeled vehicles were likely developed independently in different parts of the world, the oldest known examples come from Mesopotamia and date back to around 3500 BCE.

The development of wheeled vehicles was a significant technological advancement, but it was not without its challenges. One of the primary challenges was the need for roads that could support the weight of the vehicles. Early roads were often nothing more than dirt paths, which made travel slow and difficult. Over time, however, roads were improved and expanded to accommodate the growing number of wheeled vehicles.

The development of wheeled vehicles also had a significant impact on human societies. For example, it made it easier to transport goods over long distances, which led to the growth of trade and commerce. It also made it easier for people to travel, which led to increased cultural exchange and the spread of ideas and technologies.

One of the most significant developments in wheeled vehicles was the invention of the spoked wheel. Spoked wheels were lighter and more durable than solid wheels, and allowed for greater speed and maneuverability. They also allowed for the development of more complex vehicles, such as chariots and war wagons.

Chariots were particularly important in ancient warfare, as they allowed for rapid movement of troops and provided a mobile platform for archers and other soldiers. They were used extensively in ancient civilizations such as Egypt, Assyria, and Greece, and remained a significant part of warfare until the development of gunpowder.

The development of wheeled vehicles also had a significant impact on agriculture. The use of wheeled plows and other farm equipment made it easier to cultivate crops and increased agricultural productivity. This, in turn, led to greater food surpluses and allowed for the growth of urban centers.

Overall, the development of wheeled vehicles for animal-drawn transportation was a significant milestone in the history of human mobility. It allowed for faster and more efficient transport of goods and people, and played a significant role in the growth of trade, commerce, and urbanization. The impact of this development can still be seen today in our modern transportation systems, which continue to rely heavily on wheeled vehicles.

The Advantages and Limitations of Animal-Drawn Transportation

Animal-drawn transportation has been used by humans for thousands of years. While there are many advantages to this mode of transportation, there are also some limitations that have impacted its use over time. In this section, we will explore the advantages and limitations of animal-drawn transportation throughout history.

Advantages of Animal-Drawn Transportation

1. Access to Remote Areas: One of the primary advantages of animal-drawn transportation is that it allows people to access remote areas that would otherwise be difficult or impossible to reach. This was especially important in prehistoric times when humans were hunters and gatherers, and needed to travel long distances to find food and resources.

2. Increased Speed: Another advantage of animal-drawn transportation is that it allows people to travel faster than they would be able to on foot. This was important in ancient times when long-distance trade and travel were necessary for the development of human civilizations.

3. Increased Capacity: Animal-drawn transportation also allows for the transportation of larger loads than would

be possible on foot. This was important for agricultural societies that needed to transport crops and other goods.

4. Energy Efficiency: Animal-drawn transportation is also energy-efficient, as the animals provide the power needed to move the vehicle or load. This was important in pre-industrial times when fuel sources were limited and expensive.

Limitations of Animal-Drawn Transportation

1. Speed and Distance: While animal-drawn transportation is faster than walking, it is still relatively slow compared to other modes of transportation. This limited the range of travel and the speed at which goods could be transported.

2. Climate and Terrain: Animal-drawn transportation is also limited by climate and terrain. In areas with extreme weather conditions, such as snow or mud, animal-drawn transportation can become difficult or impossible. Similarly, rough terrain can be challenging for animals and make transportation more dangerous.

3. Animal Health and Welfare: The health and welfare of the animals used for transportation is also a limitation. Overworking animals, or using them in extreme weather conditions, can lead to injury or death.

4. Maintenance: Animal-drawn vehicles also require regular maintenance, such as replacing worn-out parts and feeding and caring for the animals. This can be time-consuming and expensive.

Conclusion

Overall, animal-drawn transportation has played a significant role in human history, providing access to remote areas, increased speed and capacity, and energy efficiency. However, it is also limited by speed and distance, climate and terrain, animal health and welfare, and maintenance. Despite these limitations, animal-drawn transportation remains an important mode of transportation in many parts of the world, and has had a lasting impact on human societies throughout history.

Chapter 2: Animal-Drawn Transportation in the Ancient World

Animal-Drawn Transportation in Mesopotamia and Egypt

The Mesopotamian and Egyptian civilizations are two of the earliest and most significant cultures in human history. They are also notable for their advancements in animal-drawn transportation, which had a profound impact on their societies and the wider world.

Mesopotamia

Mesopotamia, located in present-day Iraq, was one of the cradles of civilization, where humans first began to develop complex societies and technologies. The region was home to a number of ancient civilizations, including the Sumerians, Akkadians, Babylonians, and Assyrians, each of which contributed to the development of animal-drawn transportation.

One of the earliest examples of animal-drawn transportation in Mesopotamia was the use of donkeys and oxen to pull plows for agriculture. This allowed farmers to cultivate larger fields and produce more food, which led to the growth of urban centers and the development of trade networks.

As Mesopotamian society became more complex, animal-drawn carts and wagons were developed for transportation of goods and people. The earliest wheeled vehicles in Mesopotamia were simple carts with solid wooden wheels that were drawn by oxen or donkeys. These carts were used for short distances and were primarily used for the transportation of goods.

Later, the Mesopotamians developed more sophisticated wheeled vehicles such as chariots, which were used for both transportation and military purposes. Chariots were typically pulled by horses and were used to transport soldiers and weapons into battle. They were light, fast, and maneuverable, which made them ideal for hit-and-run tactics.

Egypt

Egypt, located in northeastern Africa, was another ancient civilization that relied heavily on animal-drawn transportation. The Nile River, which flows through Egypt, was a vital transportation route, and animal-drawn boats were used to transport goods and people up and down the river.

The Egyptians also used animals for land transportation, particularly donkeys, oxen, and horses. Donkeys were used to carry goods and people over short distances, while oxen were used for plowing and other agricultural tasks. Horses were reserved for the elite classes and were primarily used for transportation and warfare.

One of the most iconic examples of animal-drawn transportation in ancient Egypt was the use of chariots, which were primarily used for military purposes. Egyptian chariots were typically drawn by two horses and were manned by a driver and a warrior armed with a bow and arrow.

Conclusion

The use of animal-drawn transportation was a significant development in ancient Mesopotamia and Egypt, allowing for the growth of complex societies and the development of trade networks. The use of carts, wagons, and chariots revolutionized transportation and allowed goods and people to be transported more efficiently over longer distances.

The development of animal-drawn transportation in Mesopotamia and Egypt paved the way for further advancements in transportation in other parts of the world, including ancient Greece and Rome. It is a testament to the ingenuity and resourcefulness of these early civilizations, whose innovations continue to impact our lives today.

The Use of Chariots in Ancient Greece and Rome

The use of chariots in ancient Greece and Rome was a significant development in the history of animal-drawn transportation. Chariots were the preferred mode of transport for the elite in both ancient societies, and they were used for a variety of purposes, including warfare, racing, and public displays.

In ancient Greece, chariots were primarily used for racing and public displays. The earliest chariot races were held in Olympia in 680 BCE, and they quickly became a popular event at other Greek games, such as the Pythian and Isthmian games. Chariots were also used in processions, parades, and other public displays of wealth and power. They were often decorated with elaborate designs and symbols, and they served as a status symbol for the wealthy and powerful.

In ancient Rome, chariots were primarily used for warfare. Roman chariots were designed to be lightweight and maneuverable, with two wheels and a team of two or four horses. They were typically used to transport soldiers and supplies to the battlefield, and they were also used in cavalry charges. Roman chariot racing was also popular, with races held in the Circus Maximus, a massive arena that could hold up to 250,000 spectators.

Chariots were often used in battle in ancient Greece and Rome. In Greece, chariots were used primarily as a shock weapon, with the charioteer using the momentum of the chariot to charge into enemy lines. In Rome, chariots were used primarily for reconnaissance and harassment of enemy forces. They were also used in the famous chariot battles, which were mock battles between teams of charioteers.

Chariots had their advantages and disadvantages in both ancient Greece and Rome. They were fast and maneuverable, making them ideal for racing and warfare. However, they were also relatively unstable and difficult to control, making them dangerous in some situations. They were also expensive to build and maintain, which limited their availability to only the wealthiest members of society.

Despite these limitations, the use of chariots in ancient Greece and Rome had a lasting impact on the development of animal-drawn transportation. The design and technology of chariots influenced the development of other types of animal-drawn vehicles, such as carts and carriages. The use of chariots also contributed to the development of horsemanship, as charioteers had to be skilled riders and horse handlers.

In conclusion, the use of chariots in ancient Greece and Rome was a significant development in the history of animal-drawn transportation. Chariots were used for a variety of purposes, including racing, warfare, and public displays, and they had a lasting impact on the development of animal-drawn vehicles and horsemanship.

The Role of Camels and Horses in the Silk Road Trade

The Silk Road, a network of trade routes that connected China, India, and the Mediterranean world, was a vital artery of economic and cultural exchange during the ancient and medieval eras. Animal-drawn transportation played a critical role in facilitating trade along the Silk Road, with camels and horses emerging as the primary means of transport across the vast and arduous terrain.

Camels, known as the "ships of the desert," were ideally suited for long-distance travel across the arid landscapes of Central Asia and the Middle East. The Bactrian camel, with its distinctive two humps, was particularly well adapted to the harsh conditions of the Silk Road. These hardy creatures could carry heavy loads of up to 500 pounds and travel for days without water or food. They were also able to withstand extreme temperatures, ranging from scorching heat to sub-zero cold.

Horses, on the other hand, were better suited for the rugged terrain of mountainous regions such as the Himalayas and the Pamirs. The Chinese developed the famous Silk Road breed of horse, which was renowned for its speed, endurance, and agility. These horses were highly prized by traders, and were used not only for transportation but also for warfare.

The use of camels and horses in Silk Road trade had a profound impact on the economies and cultures of the regions through which they passed. The Silk Road facilitated the exchange of goods and ideas between the East and the West, and sparked the development of new industries, such as silk production in China and glass-making in the Roman Empire. The trade in luxury goods, such as silk, spices, and precious metals, enriched the coffers of the empires that controlled the trade routes, and fueled the growth of cities and trade centers along the way.

The Silk Road was not without its dangers, however. Bandits and raiders were a constant threat to travelers, and the harsh conditions of the desert and mountainous regions could be deadly. To protect themselves and their cargoes, traders formed caravans, which were often large and heavily armed. These caravans traveled in stages, stopping at designated oases or trading posts along the way to rest and resupply.

In addition to the risks posed by bandits and natural obstacles, traders on the Silk Road also faced linguistic and cultural barriers. The route passed through regions with diverse languages, religions, and customs, making communication and negotiation a challenge. To overcome these barriers, traders often relied on intermediaries who spoke multiple languages and had knowledge of local customs.

Despite the challenges, the Silk Road remained a vital trade network for over a thousand years, until the rise of sea trade in the 15th century made it less relevant. However, its legacy lives on in the form of cultural and intellectual exchange, as well as the enduring fascination with the exotic goods and tales of adventure that it inspired. The use of animal-drawn transportation played a vital role in the success of the Silk Road, and helped to shape the history of the world.

The Decline of Animal-Drawn Transportation in the Middle Ages

The Middle Ages, spanning from the 5th to the 15th century, saw a significant decline in the use of animal-drawn transportation. This decline can be attributed to several factors.

One of the major factors was the development of sea trade routes. With the advent of sea trade, transportation of goods over land became less important. Coastal cities like Venice and Genoa emerged as major trade centers due to their strategic location, and the transport of goods shifted from land to sea.

Another factor was the rise of feudalism. In feudal societies, the lords controlled most of the land and the peasants were tied to the land. This made it difficult for trade to flourish as the lords imposed taxes and tariffs on goods transported across their territories. This led to the decline of long-distance trade, which relied heavily on animal-drawn transportation.

Additionally, the widespread use of serfdom also contributed to the decline of animal-drawn transportation. Serfs were tied to the land and could not travel freely. This made it difficult to organize long-distance trade caravans as there was a lack of manpower.

The increasing use of carts and wagons during the Middle Ages also led to the decline of animal-drawn transportation. Carts and wagons were more efficient than pack animals as they could transport larger quantities of goods over longer distances. The development of better roads and bridges during this period also made it easier to transport goods by carts and wagons.

Another important factor in the decline of animal-drawn transportation was the development of gunpowder and firearms. The use of gunpowder in warfare led to the rise of standing armies and the decline of mounted knights. This, in turn, reduced the demand for horses and other pack animals.

The Black Death, a devastating pandemic that swept across Europe in the 14th century, also had a significant impact on animal-drawn transportation. The pandemic led to a shortage of labor and a decline in trade and commerce. This further reduced the demand for pack animals and carts.

In conclusion, the decline of animal-drawn transportation during the Middle Ages was a result of several factors, including the rise of sea trade routes, the development of feudalism and serfdom, the increasing use of carts and wagons, the development of gunpowder and firearms, and the impact of the Black Death. While animal-drawn transportation continued to be used in some regions, its importance as a means of transportation declined significantly during this period.

Chapter 3: The Renaissance of Animal-Drawn Transportation

The Rediscovery of Classical Learning and Culture

The Renaissance was a period of cultural, artistic, and intellectual awakening in Europe that lasted from the 14th to the 17th century. It is often considered the bridge between the Middle Ages and modern history. During this period, there was a renewed interest in the culture, art, and knowledge of classical Greece and Rome. The Renaissance was also a time of great innovation in science, technology, and transportation.

One of the key factors that contributed to the Renaissance was the rediscovery of classical learning and culture. The fall of the Western Roman Empire in the 5th century AD led to a decline in classical knowledge and culture in Europe. However, during the late Middle Ages, there was a renewed interest in the classics, particularly in Italy.

The Italian city-states of Florence, Venice, and Rome were centers of this revival, and scholars and artists flocked to these cities to study and learn from the works of ancient Greek and Roman philosophers, writers, and artists. The humanist movement, which emphasized the importance of education, rational thinking, and individualism, was also a key factor in the revival of classical learning.

The rediscovery of classical knowledge had a profound impact on transportation. The ancient Greeks and Romans had developed sophisticated transportation systems, including roads, bridges, and waterways, that were largely forgotten during the Middle Ages. However, during the Renaissance, there was a renewed interest in these systems, and they were studied, adapted, and improved upon.

One of the most important transportation innovations of the Renaissance was the development of the carriage. Carriages had been used in ancient times, but they were largely forgotten during the Middle Ages. However, during the Renaissance, carriages were rediscovered and improved upon. The carriage became a symbol of wealth and status, and it was used to transport people and goods in comfort and style.

The development of the carriage led to the improvement of roads and bridges. Roads were widened and improved, and bridges were constructed or repaired. The improvement of roads and bridges made transportation faster and more efficient, and it opened up new trade routes and markets.

The Renaissance also saw the development of new modes of transportation, such as the canal and the horse-drawn wagon. Canals were used to transport goods and people over long distances, and they were particularly important for the transport of heavy goods, such as coal and grain. Horse-drawn wagons were used to transport goods over short distances, and they were an important precursor to the modern truck.

In conclusion, the rediscovery of classical learning and culture during the Renaissance had a profound impact on transportation. It led to the development of new modes of transportation, the improvement of roads and bridges, and the revival of ancient transportation systems. The Renaissance was a time of great innovation and progress, and it laid the foundation for the modern transportation systems that we have today.

The Renaissance of Art, Science, and Technology

The Renaissance period, spanning from the 14th to the 17th century, was marked by significant cultural, intellectual, and technological advancements. During this time, there was a renewed interest in classical art, science, and technology that paved the way for the development of animal-drawn transportation.

Art

The Renaissance period is known for its art, with famous artists such as Leonardo da Vinci, Michelangelo, and Raphael creating some of the most iconic works of art in history. Art during this period was characterized by realism, perspective, and the use of light and shadow to create depth and realism. The rediscovery of classical art and techniques allowed artists to create lifelike depictions of animals and transportation, leading to more realistic and accurate portrayals of animal-drawn vehicles.

Science

The Renaissance was also a period of scientific discovery, with scientists and philosophers like Galileo, Copernicus, and Newton leading the way in the fields of astronomy, physics, and mathematics. These advancements led to a greater understanding of the laws of nature and the mechanics of motion, which had direct implications for animal-drawn transportation. For example, Galileo's work on motion and inertia helped engineers create more efficient and stable animal-drawn vehicles.

Technology

Technological advancements during the Renaissance period also played a significant role in the development of animal-drawn transportation. The invention of the printing press allowed for the dissemination of knowledge on a mass scale, leading to increased knowledge sharing and innovation. Improved metallurgy techniques allowed for the creation of stronger, lighter, and more durable materials, such as steel and iron, which were used in the construction of animal-drawn vehicles. The development of the wheel and axle, which had been used since ancient times, was improved upon during the Renaissance, allowing for more efficient and faster transportation.

In addition to these advancements, the Renaissance period also saw the development of new types of animal-drawn vehicles. Carriages, for example, became more elaborate and were used to transport people in luxury and comfort. These carriages were often pulled by horses and were a common sight in cities and towns throughout Europe. Wagon technology also improved during this period, with the introduction of the spring wagon, which had a suspension system that made for a smoother ride.

Conclusion

The Renaissance period marked a significant turning point in the history of animal-drawn transportation. The renewed interest in classical learning and culture, coupled with scientific and technological advancements, led to a period of innovation and growth in this field. The use of animal-drawn vehicles became more efficient, comfortable, and reliable, making transportation more accessible and practical for people across Europe. The advancements made during this period would lay the foundation for future transportation innovations and technologies.

The Role of Animal-Drawn Transportation in Renaissance Society

The Renaissance was a period of cultural and intellectual rebirth that spanned from the 14th to the 17th century in Europe. It was marked by a renewed interest in the classical world and an explosion of creativity in the arts, sciences, and technology. This era also saw a resurgence in the use of animal-drawn transportation, particularly in urban settings. In this section, we will explore the role of animal-drawn transportation in Renaissance society.

The Renaissance was a time of great change and progress, and animal-drawn transportation played an important role in the growth and development of cities. Horses, mules, and oxen were used to transport goods and people throughout the cities and countryside, and carts and carriages became a common sight on the streets. These modes of transportation were particularly important for trade, as they allowed goods to be transported quickly and efficiently between different markets.

In Renaissance Italy, horses and carriages were used not only for transportation but also as a symbol of status and power. Wealthy individuals would often ride in elaborately decorated carriages with ornate designs and painted coats of arms. These carriages were a display of wealth and social standing, and owning one was a sign of prestige.

The rise of animal-drawn transportation also had a significant impact on the economy. The increased use of carts and carriages meant that more goods could be transported more quickly and efficiently, leading to increased trade and commerce. This led to the growth of industries such as blacksmithing, harness making, and wheelwrighting, which were all necessary for the production and maintenance of carts and carriages.

The use of animal-drawn transportation also had social and cultural implications. The availability of carts and carriages made it easier for people to travel to different parts of the city, attend events, and visit friends and family. This helped to break down the barriers between different social classes, as people of all backgrounds could now travel more easily and interact with each other.

Animal-drawn transportation also had an impact on the environment. As more and more carts and carriages filled the streets, the roads became increasingly crowded and dirty. This led to a need for improved road infrastructure, including the paving of streets and the construction of bridges and tunnels. These developments not only made transportation easier but also helped to improve sanitation and hygiene in urban areas.

In conclusion, the Renaissance saw a resurgence in the use of animal-drawn transportation, particularly in urban areas. Horses, mules, and oxen were used to transport goods and people throughout the cities and countryside, and carts and carriages became a common sight on the streets. The rise of animal-drawn transportation had significant economic, social, and cultural implications, and helped to shape the world we live in today.

The Evolution of Carriages and Coaches

The Renaissance period marked a significant evolution in animal-drawn transportation, particularly in the development of carriages and coaches. During this time, the use of carriages and coaches became a symbol of status and luxury among the aristocracy and wealthy classes, leading to the creation of increasingly elaborate and ornate designs.

One of the earliest and most basic forms of carriages during the Renaissance period was the one-horse chaise. This simple carriage featured a lightweight design and could accommodate one or two passengers, making it ideal for personal use. Another popular carriage during this time was the four-wheeled coach, which could accommodate multiple passengers and was often used for public transport or for long-distance travel.

As the Renaissance period progressed, carriages and coaches became more elaborate and ornate in design. One notable example was the "Gig," a light two-wheeled carriage with a high front seat and a low back seat. This type of carriage was popular for leisurely rides through parks or gardens, and often featured intricate carvings and decorations.

Another notable carriage from this period was the "Berline," a four-wheeled coach with an enclosed passenger compartment and a separate driver's seat. The Berline was often used for travel by wealthy individuals, and its elaborate design included a folding roof and curtains for privacy.

The Renaissance period also saw significant advancements in carriage and coach technology. The suspension system, for example, was greatly improved, with the development of a more sophisticated system that could absorb shocks and provide a smoother ride. In addition, improvements were made to the brakes, making them more effective and reliable.

The evolution of carriages and coaches during the Renaissance period was not limited to design and technology. The way in which they were used and perceived also changed significantly. As the use of carriages and coaches became more widespread, they became a symbol of social status and luxury. Those who could afford to ride in carriages and coaches were seen as belonging to the upper class and were often admired by others.

In conclusion, the Renaissance period was a time of significant evolution in animal-drawn transportation, particularly in the development of carriages and coaches. From simple one-horse chaises to ornate four-wheeled coaches, the designs became increasingly elaborate and ornate. Advancements in technology such as the suspension system and brakes made them more reliable and comfortable. The use of carriages and coaches became a symbol of social status and luxury, and they were often admired by others.

Chapter 4: The Age of Horse-Drawn Transportation
The Industrial Revolution and the Rise of the Horse-Drawn Carriage

The Industrial Revolution was a significant period in history, marked by a rapid increase in technological advancement and manufacturing production. With the rise of factories and industries, transportation systems also evolved to keep pace with the demands of the changing times. The horse-drawn carriage played a crucial role in this era of transportation, enabling goods and people to move more efficiently and quickly than ever before.

The Industrial Revolution and Transportation:

The Industrial Revolution saw a transformation in manufacturing, production, and transportation systems. The development of machines and steam power allowed goods to be produced on a massive scale, leading to a surge in demand for efficient transportation.

During this period, the horse-drawn carriage became the primary mode of transportation for both goods and people. Carriages were widely used for transporting goods from factories to markets, while personal carriages became a symbol of wealth and social status. The rise of the middle class in urban areas also contributed to an increase in the demand for horse-drawn transportation.

Horse-Drawn Carriages and Their Types:

Horse-drawn carriages came in various types, each designed for a specific purpose. The most common types were:

1. Stagecoaches: These were large carriages that could carry multiple passengers and were mainly used for long-distance travel.

2. Hacks: These were small carriages that could accommodate two passengers and were commonly used for short-distance travel.

3. Broughams: These were four-wheeled carriages that were closed at the sides and had a glass window at the front.

4. Landau: These were four-wheeled carriages with a convertible roof that could be opened or closed depending on the weather.

The Impact of the Horse-Drawn Carriage:

The horse-drawn carriage played a significant role in the Industrial Revolution by improving transportation systems, making it possible to transport goods and people more efficiently. The carriages were faster and more comfortable than previous transportation options, such as carts or wagons.

Moreover, the horse-drawn carriage created jobs in various areas, including carriage making, harness making, and horse breeding. The demand for horses increased significantly, and breeding them became a lucrative business. Horse-drawn carriages also opened up new opportunities for tourism, as people could travel to new destinations more quickly and comfortably.

The End of the Horse-Drawn Carriage Era:

Despite their popularity and success, the horse-drawn carriages' reign eventually came to an end with the introduction of motorized vehicles. The first automobiles were introduced in the late 1800s and quickly replaced horse-drawn carriages as the primary mode of transportation. The decline of the horse-drawn carriage industry had a significant impact on the economy and society, leading to job losses and a shift in transportation culture.

Conclusion:

The horse-drawn carriage played a crucial role in the Industrial Revolution, providing an efficient means of transportation for goods and people. The carriages' impact on the economy and society was significant, creating new job opportunities and contributing to the rise of the middle class. However, with the introduction of motorized vehicles, the horse-drawn carriage era came to an end, marking the beginning of a new era in transportation history.

The Importance of Horses in Agriculture and Trade

Introduction: Horses have played a significant role in transportation, agriculture, and trade for thousands of years. In the Age of Horse-Drawn Transportation, they were particularly important in moving people and goods across long distances. This chapter explores the importance of horses in agriculture and trade during this period.

The Importance of Horses in Agriculture: Horses were the primary source of power for agricultural work until the late 19th century. Horses were used for plowing, harrowing, and hauling goods. The use of horses in agriculture increased productivity, allowing farmers to cultivate larger areas of land and produce more crops.

In the United States, the use of horses in agriculture peaked in the late 19th century. The introduction of tractors in the early 20th century led to the decline in the use of horses in agriculture. However, horses continued to be used for some agricultural tasks, such as planting and harvesting crops in narrow rows.

The Importance of Horses in Trade: Horses were also critical in trade during the Age of Horse-Drawn Transportation. Horses were used to transport goods over long distances, particularly in regions where water transport was not available. Horses were used to pull wagons and carriages carrying goods such as textiles, lumber, and foodstuffs.

Horses were essential to the delivery of mail and newspapers. Horse-drawn stagecoaches were used to transport people and mail across the United States in the 19th century. The Pony Express used a network of horse relays to deliver mail between Missouri and California in just 10 days.

In cities, horses were used to pull streetcars and omnibuses. Horse-drawn omnibuses were the primary mode of transportation in cities until the introduction of the electric streetcar in the late 19th century.

Challenges of Using Horses in Transportation: While horses were an essential component of transportation and agriculture, their use was not without challenges. The availability of horses was limited by their cost, breeding, and training. Horses required significant care and feeding, making their maintenance costly.

The use of horses in transportation also had significant environmental impacts. Horse manure and urine were a significant source of pollution in cities, leading to the spread of diseases such as cholera and typhoid fever. The use of horses in transportation also led to the degradation of roads, particularly in cities where heavy traffic was concentrated.

Conclusion: Horses played a vital role in agriculture and trade during the Age of Horse-Drawn Transportation. The use of horses in agriculture increased productivity, while their use in transportation facilitated trade and communication. Despite the challenges associated with their use, horses were an essential part of daily life for many people during this period.

The Advent of Streetcars and Omnibuses

The invention of streetcars and omnibuses was a significant development in the history of transportation. Prior to their introduction, horse-drawn vehicles were the primary mode of public transportation in cities. The advent of streetcars and omnibuses provided a more efficient and comfortable way for people to travel within cities. In this section, we will explore the history of these vehicles and their impact on society.

The History of Streetcars:

The first streetcar was invented in the early 19th century. It was a horse-drawn vehicle that ran on tracks laid in the streets. The tracks made it possible for the streetcar to travel faster and more smoothly than other horse-drawn vehicles. The first streetcar lines were established in the United States, but the concept quickly spread to other countries.

By the mid-19th century, streetcars were a common sight in many American cities. They were used to transport people to work, shopping, and entertainment venues. In some cities, streetcars were even used to transport goods and materials. The popularity of streetcars led to the development of new technologies to improve their speed and comfort.

One of the most significant developments was the introduction of cable cars. Cable cars were powered by a cable that ran beneath the street. The cable was driven by a large steam engine, which provided power to the cable. The cable allowed the streetcar to travel much faster than a horse-drawn vehicle and made it possible to climb steep hills.

The History of Omnibuses:

Omnibuses were another important development in the history of transportation. They were horse-drawn vehicles that were larger and more comfortable than other horse-drawn vehicles. Omnibuses were used for public transportation and could carry up to 12 passengers.

The first omnibus was introduced in Paris in 1828. It was quickly adopted in other European cities and then in North America. In the United States, omnibuses were used primarily in urban areas. They were used to transport people between neighborhoods and to connect people to other forms of transportation, such as ferries and railroads.

Omnibuses were an important step forward in public transportation because they provided a more comfortable and reliable way to travel. They were also more efficient than other horse-drawn vehicles because they could carry more passengers at once.

The Impact of Streetcars and Omnibuses:

The introduction of streetcars and omnibuses had a significant impact on society. They made it easier for people to travel within cities, which led to the growth of cities and the development of new suburbs. They also made it possible for people to live further away from their workplaces, which led to the development of commuter towns.

Streetcars and omnibuses were also important for social and cultural reasons. They made it possible for people to travel to theaters, museums, and other entertainment venues. They also made it possible for people to connect with others from different parts of the city.

Conclusion:

In conclusion, the introduction of streetcars and omnibuses was a significant development in the history of transportation. These vehicles provided a more efficient and comfortable way for people to travel within cities. They also had a significant impact on the growth and development of cities, as well as on social and cultural life. Although they have been largely replaced by other forms of transportation, their legacy lives on in the modern transportation systems we use today.

The Impact of Horse-Drawn Transportation on Urbanization

Introduction: Horse-drawn transportation had a significant impact on urbanization in the 19th century. It enabled people and goods to move faster and more efficiently, which facilitated the growth of cities. This section will explore the impact of horse-drawn transportation on urbanization and the various factors that contributed to the growth of cities during this time.

The Growth of Cities: During the 19th century, the growth of cities was primarily driven by industrialization. As industries developed, cities became centers of trade and commerce. The growth of cities was also fueled by immigration, as people moved from rural areas to urban centers in search of employment opportunities.

Horse-Drawn Transportation: Horse-drawn transportation played a crucial role in the growth of cities during this period. It enabled people and goods to move faster and more efficiently, which made cities more accessible. Horse-drawn carriages, streetcars, and omnibuses were the primary modes of transportation in the 19th century.

Horse-Drawn Carriages: Horse-drawn carriages were popular among the wealthy and were primarily used for private transportation. They were often used for leisure activities such as promenading and visiting friends. They were also used for business purposes such as transporting goods and conducting meetings.

Streetcars: Streetcars were first introduced in the early 19th century and quickly became a popular mode of transportation in cities. They were cheaper than horse-drawn carriages and were accessible to a wider range of people. They were also faster and more efficient than horse-drawn carriages.

Omnibuses: Omnibuses were introduced in the mid-19th century and were essentially larger versions of stagecoaches. They were able to transport larger numbers of people and were a cheaper alternative to private transportation. They were used primarily for public transportation and were an important factor in the growth of cities.

The Impact of Horse-Drawn Transportation on Urbanization: Horse-drawn transportation had a significant impact on urbanization in the 19th century. It made it easier for people to travel and allowed goods to be transported more efficiently. This facilitated the growth of cities as people were able to move to urban centers in search of employment opportunities. Horse-drawn transportation also contributed to the development of suburbs, as people were able to live further away from their place of work and still have access to transportation.

Horse-drawn transportation also had a significant impact on the layout of cities. It enabled the development of transportation networks such as streetcar lines, which encouraged the growth of suburbs and allowed people to move farther away from the city center. This led to the development of a radial pattern of growth, where cities grew outward from their center in a circular pattern.

Conclusion: Horse-drawn transportation played a crucial role in the growth of cities during the 19th century. It enabled people and goods to move faster and more efficiently, which facilitated the growth of urban centers. Horse-drawn carriages, streetcars, and omnibuses were the primary modes of transportation during this period and had a significant impact on the layout of cities. The development of transportation networks enabled the growth of suburbs and the development of a radial pattern of growth. Overall, the impact of horse-drawn transportation on urbanization cannot be overstated.

Chapter 5: The Limits of Animal-Drawn Transportation

The Environmental and Social Costs of Animal-Drawn Transportation

Introduction Animal-drawn transportation has played a vital role in human history, but it has also had its limitations and drawbacks. As human society has progressed, the environmental and social costs of animal-drawn transportation have become increasingly apparent. In this chapter, we will explore these costs and discuss the need to find more sustainable and efficient alternatives to animal-drawn transportation.

Environmental Costs of Animal-Drawn Transportation Animal-drawn transportation has a significant impact on the environment, particularly in terms of land use, greenhouse gas emissions, and air and water pollution. The following sections will discuss each of these in detail.

Land Use One of the significant environmental costs of animal-drawn transportation is the amount of land required to support the animals. This land is typically used for grazing and growing crops to feed the animals. In many parts of the world, the demand for land for animal husbandry has led to deforestation and the conversion of natural habitats into agricultural land.

Greenhouse Gas Emissions Animal-drawn transportation is a significant contributor to greenhouse gas emissions, particularly methane and carbon dioxide. These emissions are primarily a result of animal digestion and manure decomposition. The emissions from animal husbandry and transportation account for approximately 14.5% of global greenhouse gas emissions, making it a significant contributor to climate change.

Air and Water Pollution Animal husbandry and transportation also have a significant impact on air and water quality. The production and transportation of animal feed can result in air pollution, and the runoff from animal waste can pollute waterways and groundwater.

Social Costs of Animal-Drawn Transportation In addition to the environmental costs, animal-drawn transportation also has social costs, particularly in terms of animal welfare, human health, and economic inequality.

Animal Welfare The use of animals for transportation can lead to animal abuse and neglect. Animals used for transportation are often overworked, underfed, and subjected to harsh living conditions. This mistreatment can result in injury, illness, and premature death.

Human Health The close proximity of animals in transportation can also pose a health risk to humans. Diseases such as anthrax, brucellosis, and Q fever can be transmitted from animals to humans, putting the health of animal handlers and consumers of animal products at risk.

Economic Inequality The use of animal-drawn transportation can also perpetuate economic inequality. In many parts of the world, animal husbandry and transportation are labor-intensive and require significant capital investment. This makes it difficult for small-scale farmers and businesses to compete with large-scale industrial operations.

Conclusion While animal-drawn transportation has played an important role in human history, it has also had significant environmental and social costs. As human society continues to evolve, it is essential to find more sustainable and efficient alternatives to animal-drawn transportation. This will require a concerted effort from governments, businesses, and individuals to promote more sustainable modes of transportation and to reduce the reliance on animal husbandry and transportation.

The Health and Welfare of Animals Used in Transportation

The use of animals for transportation has been an important aspect of human civilization for thousands of years. Horses, camels, oxen, and other animals have been used for a wide range of transportation purposes, from carrying goods and people to pulling plows and other farm equipment. However, the use of animals for transportation has been controversial throughout history, and concerns about the health and welfare of the animals used in transportation have been raised by animal welfare advocates and others.

One of the primary concerns about the use of animals in transportation is the physical toll that it can take on the animals themselves. Horses and other animals used in transportation are often subjected to long hours of work in challenging environmental conditions, such as extreme heat or cold, and may be forced to work without adequate rest or food. This can result in a range of physical ailments, including fatigue, dehydration, and musculoskeletal injuries. In addition, animals may be subjected to harsh treatment by their handlers, which can cause psychological distress and further exacerbate their physical ailments.

Another concern is the social and environmental impact of animal transportation. Animal-drawn vehicles can generate significant amounts of pollution, including dust and emissions from manure, which can be harmful to both animals and humans. In addition, the use of animals for transportation can contribute to deforestation and other environmental problems, as land is cleared to create pasture for animals and to grow crops to feed them. This can result in soil erosion, loss of biodiversity, and other environmental problems.

Animal welfare advocates have long been concerned about the health and welfare of animals used in transportation. They argue that animals are sentient beings with the ability to experience pain and suffering, and that they should be treated with respect and compassion. Animal welfare advocates have called for increased regulation of animal transportation, including the use of humane transport methods and the provision of adequate food, water, and rest for animals in transit.

Governments and other organizations have also taken steps to address the health and welfare of animals used in transportation. In many countries, regulations have been put in place to ensure that animals are treated humanely during transportation, and to protect them from abuse and neglect.

These regulations may include requirements for the provision of adequate food, water, and rest for animals, as well as restrictions on the amount of time that animals can be transported without a break.

Animal welfare advocates have also called for increased research into the health and welfare of animals used in transportation. This research could help to identify best practices for animal transportation, and to develop new technologies and methods for improving the health and welfare of animals in transit. For example, new materials and designs for animal transportation equipment could be developed that are more comfortable and less stressful for animals, while also reducing the environmental impact of animal transportation.

In conclusion, concerns about the health and welfare of animals used in transportation have been raised by animal welfare advocates and others for many years. While animal transportation has played an important role in human civilization for thousands of years, it is important to consider the physical, social, and environmental costs of this practice. Increased regulation, research, and innovation may be needed to ensure that animal transportation is conducted in a humane and sustainable manner, while also meeting the needs of human society.

The Challenges of Maintenance, Fuel, and Speed

Introduction: Animal-drawn transportation has been an integral part of human civilization for centuries. However, despite its many advantages, it has its limitations. One of the major challenges of animal-drawn transportation is maintenance, fuel, and speed. In this chapter, we will explore the various challenges associated with maintaining animal-drawn transportation and the limitations of fuel and speed.

Maintenance of Animal-Drawn Transportation: Maintenance of animal-drawn transportation can be a challenging task. Animals used for transportation are subjected to constant wear and tear, which can lead to various problems like injury, illness, and exhaustion. To prevent such problems, regular maintenance and care of animals are necessary.

Regular veterinary checkups are essential for the health of animals used for transportation. In addition, proper nutrition, rest, and exercise are critical for the well-being of these animals. Lack of proper care and maintenance can lead to a decline in the health of animals, which can impact their performance and, ultimately, the efficiency of transportation.

The maintenance of wagons and carriages is equally important. The constant use of these vehicles can lead to wear and tear, which can impact their functionality. Regular maintenance and repair are necessary to ensure that the wagons and carriages are in good working condition.

Fuel Limitations: The limitations of fuel can impact animal-drawn transportation in various ways. The primary fuel used for animal-drawn transportation is hay, oats, and other grains. However, the availability of such fuels can be limited, especially during periods of drought or crop failure.

In addition, the cost of fuel can fluctuate, making it difficult for some people to afford. This can lead to a decline in the use of animal-drawn transportation, as people opt for other forms of transportation that are more affordable and accessible.

Speed Limitations: One of the major limitations of animal-drawn transportation is speed. The speed of animal-drawn transportation is limited by the speed of the animals pulling the wagons and carriages. The average speed of a horse-drawn carriage is around 5-10 miles per hour, depending on the terrain and weather conditions.

This limitation can impact the efficiency of transportation, especially in emergencies or situations where time is of the essence. It can also impact the competitiveness of animal-drawn transportation, as other forms of transportation like trains and automobiles can travel much faster.

Conclusion: In conclusion, maintenance, fuel, and speed are some of the major challenges associated with animal-drawn transportation. The proper maintenance and care of animals used for transportation, as well as regular maintenance and repair of wagons and carriages, are essential to ensure the efficient functioning of animal-drawn transportation.

The limitations of fuel availability and cost, as well as the speed limitations of animal-drawn transportation, can impact its efficiency and competitiveness. However, despite these challenges, animal-drawn transportation remains an important mode of transportation in some parts of the world, and efforts to address these challenges are ongoing.

The Rise of Competition from Steam and Internal Combustion Engines

The rise of steam and internal combustion engines in the late 19th and early 20th centuries posed a significant challenge to animal-drawn transportation. These new technologies promised greater speed, efficiency, and reliability than animal-drawn vehicles, and they quickly began to replace them in many areas.

Steam power, in particular, had a significant impact on transportation. The development of steam engines made it possible to power trains, steamships, and even automobiles. These new modes of transportation could travel much faster and over longer distances than animal-drawn vehicles, and they quickly became the preferred choice for many people.

Steam-powered trains, in particular, revolutionized transportation in the 19th century. They were much faster and more efficient than animal-drawn vehicles, and they made it possible to transport goods and people over long distances quickly and cheaply. As a result, many companies began to shift their focus away from animal-drawn transportation and towards steam-powered transportation.

The internal combustion engine, which was first developed in the late 19th century, had an even greater impact on transportation. It made it possible to power cars, trucks, and buses, and it quickly began to replace horse-drawn carriages and carts in many cities. Internal combustion engines were much more efficient and reliable than horses, and they could travel much faster and over longer distances.

The rise of these new technologies posed a significant challenge to animal-drawn transportation. Animal-drawn vehicles were no longer the fastest, most efficient, or most reliable form of transportation, and they began to fall out of favor in many areas. This shift had a significant impact on the people who relied on animal-drawn transportation for their livelihoods, and many were forced to adapt to the new reality or face financial ruin.

Despite the challenges posed by steam and internal combustion engines, animal-drawn transportation continued to play an important role in some areas. In many rural areas, for example, animal-drawn vehicles remained the most practical and economical form of transportation well into the 20th century. And in some urban areas, animal-drawn vehicles continued to play a role in certain industries, such as waste management and construction.

Overall, however, the rise of steam and internal combustion engines marked the beginning of the end for animal-drawn transportation. While horses and other draft animals continued to play an important role in some areas for many years, they were gradually replaced by newer, more efficient technologies. Today, animal-drawn transportation is mostly a relic of the past, remembered only in history books and the occasional parade or festival.

Chapter 6: The Legacy of Animal-Drawn Transportation

The Enduring Symbolism of Horse-Drawn Carriages

Introduction: Horse-drawn carriages have played a significant role in transportation history and continue to evoke a sense of nostalgia and romanticism. From fairy tales to royal weddings, they have been a part of cultural celebrations worldwide. This chapter explores the legacy of animal-drawn transportation, focusing on the enduring symbolism of horse-drawn carriages.

Historical Significance: Horse-drawn carriages were once the primary mode of transportation for the wealthy and elite. They were used to attend social events, travel to work, and transport goods. Carriages were also a symbol of status and power, with different types of carriages used for different occasions. The Victoria carriage, for example, was reserved for formal events and was pulled by a team of four horses.

Nostalgia and Romance: The romanticized image of a horse-drawn carriage often conjures up images of fairy tales and love stories. Cinderella's pumpkin carriage and the carriage ride in "Gone with the Wind" are just a few examples of how carriages have been used to create romantic settings in popular culture. Horse-drawn carriages are also a popular choice for weddings, with many couples choosing to arrive at their ceremony in a carriage, adding to the fairy tale atmosphere.

Tourism: In many cities worldwide, horse-drawn carriages are still used as a tourist attraction. Tourists can enjoy a scenic ride through city streets or historic sites, with knowledgeable guides providing a historical and cultural context. In some cases, carriages are decorated with festive lights or flowers to add to the tourist experience.

Controversy: Despite their cultural significance, horse-drawn carriages have been the subject of controversy. Animal rights activists argue that the horses used to pull carriages are mistreated and overworked, leading to health problems and a shorter lifespan. In some cities, laws have been passed to regulate the use of horse-drawn carriages, while others have banned them altogether.

Conclusion: The legacy of animal-drawn transportation, particularly horse-drawn carriages, continues to be felt today. While they are no longer the primary mode of transportation, they remain an enduring symbol of nostalgia, romance, and cultural significance. As technology continues to advance, it is important to preserve the historical and cultural significance of horse-drawn carriages, while also addressing concerns regarding animal welfare.

The Preservation and Restoration of Antique Carriages

The history of animal-drawn transportation has left an indelible mark on human civilization. From the earliest days of human history to the present, animals have played a crucial role in moving people and goods. In the modern era, however, the dominance of animal-drawn transportation has been replaced by automobiles, airplanes, and other forms of transportation.

Despite this, the legacy of animal-drawn transportation lives on, and one aspect of this legacy is the preservation and restoration of antique carriages. Antique carriages are a tangible link to the past, a reminder of a time when transportation was slower and more leisurely, and they offer insights into the lives of the people who used them.

The preservation and restoration of antique carriages is a specialized field that combines the expertise of historians, art conservators, and craftsmen. There are a number of organizations and individuals around the world who are dedicated to this work, and their efforts have helped to ensure that these historical artifacts remain accessible to future generations.

One of the key challenges in preserving and restoring antique carriages is the fact that they were often made using materials and techniques that are no longer widely used. Many antique carriages were made with materials such as wood, leather, and brass, which can deteriorate over time. In addition, the craftsmanship required to make many of these carriages is no longer widely practiced.

To address these challenges, preservationists and restorers use a combination of traditional and modern techniques. For example, they may use computer-aided design (CAD) software to create digital models of carriages, which can then be used to create accurate replicas. They may also use modern materials and techniques to repair or replace damaged parts.

In addition to the technical challenges of preservation and restoration, there are also ethical and aesthetic considerations. Many antique carriages were designed and built at a time when animal welfare was not a priority, and it is important for modern preservationists to take this into account. This may involve replacing leather harnesses with synthetic materials, or making modifications to the carriage to ensure the comfort and safety of the horses.

Another consideration is the aesthetic value of antique carriages. Many of these carriages are works of art in their own right, and it is important to preserve their unique beauty and character. This may involve using traditional techniques to restore or replicate decorative elements such as carvings, paintings, or gilding.

Preservation and restoration efforts for antique carriages can take many forms. Some organizations focus on the restoration of individual carriages, while others work to create collections of carriages that are open to the public. In some cases, antique carriages are used for special events such as weddings or parades, providing a unique and memorable experience for participants and spectators alike.

The preservation and restoration of antique carriages is not only important for historical and cultural reasons but also for the insights they provide into the development of transportation technology. Antique carriages represent an important transitional period in transportation history, marking the shift from animal-drawn transportation to the modern era of automobiles and other motorized vehicles.

In conclusion, the preservation and restoration of antique carriages is an important aspect of the legacy of animal-drawn transportation. Through these efforts, we can gain a greater appreciation for the craftsmanship, beauty, and historical significance of these artifacts. By ensuring their preservation, we can ensure that future generations can continue to learn from and be inspired by them.

The Continued Use of Animals for Transportation in Developing Countries

Introduction: Animal transportation, specifically with the use of horses, mules, and oxen, was once a significant form of transportation worldwide. However, with the development of new technology and industrialization, animal-drawn transportation has become less common in developed countries. Nevertheless, it continues to be used in many developing countries as an inexpensive and accessible mode of transportation. In this section, we will discuss the continued use of animals for transportation in developing countries.

Animal Transport in Developing Countries: Animal transportation is still a prevalent mode of transportation in developing countries due to economic reasons. Many people in these countries cannot afford to purchase cars, trucks, or other modern forms of transportation, and animal transportation is a much cheaper option. Furthermore, animals are often available locally and require less infrastructure and maintenance costs than modern vehicles.

Uses of Animal Transportation: Animals are commonly used for various transportation needs in developing countries, including the transportation of people, goods, and agricultural produce. In rural areas, animals are still used to transport farming equipment, such as plows and carts, which are often too heavy or bulky for human transport. Additionally, animals are used to transport goods and agricultural produce to local markets, where they can be sold for income. Animal transport is also used to transport people in rural areas where there is no public transportation or private vehicles available.

Challenges and Issues: Although animal transport continues to be used in many developing countries, it is not without challenges and issues. One of the main challenges is the welfare of the animals. Many animals used for transportation are overworked, underfed, and lack proper shelter. This can lead to injuries, illness, and even death. There is also a concern about the environmental impact of animal transport, including the contribution to greenhouse gases, pollution, and damage to local ecosystems.

Efforts to Improve Animal Welfare: Several organizations and governments are working to improve the welfare of animals used in transportation in developing countries. These efforts include education and training programs for animal owners, improved animal healthcare services, and the development of better transportation equipment for animals. Additionally, some organizations are working to develop alternative transportation options that are more environmentally friendly and sustainable.

Conclusion: The continued use of animals for transportation in developing countries highlights the importance of animal-drawn transportation as a cultural, social, and economic practice. However, it also underscores the challenges and issues associated with this practice. As we move towards a more sustainable and environmentally conscious future, it is essential to find ways to balance the cultural and economic importance of animal transportation with the welfare of the animals and the environment.

The Lessons of Animal-Drawn Transportation for Modern Mobility

Animal-drawn transportation played a crucial role in human history, providing a means of transportation for people and goods for thousands of years. Despite its decline in the modern era, there are still many lessons that can be learned from the use of animals for transportation, which can be applied to modern mobility solutions. In this section, we will explore some of these lessons and their relevance to modern transportation.

Sustainability and Environmental Impact

One of the most important lessons from animal-drawn transportation is the importance of sustainability and minimizing environmental impact. Animals are a renewable resource, and they have a much lower environmental impact than fossil fuel-based transportation. They do not emit greenhouse gases, and their waste can be used as fertilizer. In contrast, fossil fuel-based transportation is a major contributor to air pollution, which has significant health and environmental impacts.

In the modern era, there has been a growing awareness of the importance of sustainability and minimizing environmental impact. Electric vehicles, public transportation, and other alternative modes of transportation have become increasingly popular, as people seek to reduce their carbon footprint and mitigate the impacts of climate change. By drawing on the lessons of animal-drawn transportation, we can continue to develop more sustainable and environmentally-friendly transportation solutions.

Efficiency and Reliability

Another lesson from animal-drawn transportation is the importance of efficiency and reliability. Animals were highly efficient and reliable means of transportation, able to cover long distances with minimal maintenance and repair. In contrast, fossil fuel-based transportation is often less efficient and more prone to breakdowns and malfunctions.

Efficiency and reliability are also important considerations in modern transportation. Public transportation systems, for example, must be designed to maximize efficiency and minimize delays, while also ensuring that they are reliable and can operate safely and effectively. By drawing on the lessons of animal-drawn transportation, we can develop more efficient and reliable transportation solutions that meet the needs of modern society.

Accessibility and Affordability

Animal-drawn transportation was often more accessible and affordable than other forms of transportation. For many people, animals provided a means of transportation that they could afford and access, even if they were not able to afford more expensive forms of transportation.

Accessibility and affordability remain important considerations in modern transportation. Public transportation systems must be designed to be accessible to people with disabilities and people of all income levels, to ensure that everyone has access to safe and reliable transportation. By drawing on the lessons of animal-drawn transportation, we can develop transportation solutions that are more accessible and affordable for everyone.

Community and Culture

Finally, animal-drawn transportation was often closely tied to community and culture. Animals were often raised and cared for within local communities, and their use for transportation was often part of local traditions and cultures. This helped to strengthen community ties and create a sense of shared identity and heritage.

Community and culture remain important considerations in modern transportation. Public transportation systems, for example, can help to bring people together and create a sense of shared identity and purpose. By drawing on the lessons of animal-drawn transportation, we can develop transportation solutions that foster community and cultural connections.

Conclusion

The lessons of animal-drawn transportation are still relevant today, as we seek to develop more sustainable, efficient, reliable, accessible, and culturally-relevant transportation solutions. By drawing on the strengths and advantages of animal-drawn transportation, we can create a better future for ourselves and for future generations.

Chapter 7: The Future of Animal-Drawn Transportation

The Emergence of Sustainable and Ethical Animal-Drawn Transportation

As the world becomes increasingly conscious of sustainability and animal welfare, there is a growing interest in finding ways to make animal-drawn transportation more ethical and sustainable. While animal-drawn transportation may seem like an outdated mode of transportation, it still has a place in certain communities, particularly in developing countries where access to modern transportation is limited. In this chapter, we will explore the emergence of sustainable and ethical animal-drawn transportation and the ways in which it can be integrated into modern transportation systems.

The Importance of Sustainable and Ethical Animal-Drawn Transportation In many developing countries, animal-drawn transportation plays a critical role in daily life. From transporting goods to carrying people to marketplaces or healthcare facilities, animal-drawn transportation provides a vital service in many communities. However, it is also true that the use of animals in transportation can have negative impacts on animal welfare, human health, and the environment. The emergence of sustainable and ethical animal-drawn transportation is, therefore, of utmost importance.

Sustainable Animal-Drawn Transportation Sustainable animal-drawn transportation refers to the use of animals in transportation in a way that minimizes negative impacts on the environment, animal welfare, and human health. This can be achieved in a number of ways. For example, using lightweight and efficient carts, harnesses, and other equipment can reduce the physical burden on animals, allowing them to work for longer periods without suffering from exhaustion or injury. In addition, training animal owners and drivers in proper animal care and management can help to ensure that animals are treated humanely and are not subjected to unnecessary suffering.

Ethical Animal-Drawn Transportation Ethical animal-drawn transportation goes beyond sustainability to consider the broader ethical implications of using animals in transportation. This includes ensuring that animals are treated humanely, that their welfare is monitored and protected, and that they are not subjected to unnecessary suffering. It also involves ensuring that animal owners and drivers are educated in proper animal care and management.

Modernizing Animal-Drawn Transportation While animal-drawn transportation may seem like an outdated mode of transportation, there are ways to modernize it and make it more sustainable and ethical. For example, using electric or hybrid carts, harnesses, and other equipment can reduce the physical burden on animals while also reducing emissions and improving air quality. In addition, using GPS technology and other modern tools can help animal owners and drivers optimize their routes, reducing travel time and distance while also minimizing the physical burden on animals.

Integrating Animal-Drawn Transportation into Modern Transportation Systems To ensure the continued use of animal-drawn transportation in a sustainable and ethical manner, it is essential to integrate it into modern transportation systems. This can involve working with governments and other organizations to develop regulations and guidelines for the use of animals in transportation, as well as providing training and education for animal owners and drivers. In addition, developing infrastructure to support animal-drawn transportation, such as dedicated lanes or paths, can help to improve safety and reduce the risk of accidents.

Conclusion While the use of animals in transportation may seem like an outdated practice, it still plays a critical role in many communities around the world. By modernizing animal-drawn transportation and making it more sustainable and ethical, we can ensure that it continues to provide a valuable service while also protecting animal welfare, human health, and the environment. Through continued research, education, and innovation, we can create a future where animal-drawn transportation is a sustainable and ethical mode of transportation for all.

The Use of Animal-Drawn Transportation in Tourism and Recreation

Introduction: Animal-drawn transportation has been an essential means of transportation for centuries. Even though it has been replaced by other modes of transportation, it remains an important part of tourism and recreation, especially in areas with a rich cultural heritage. The use of animal-drawn transportation can provide a unique and sustainable experience for tourists while generating income for local communities. In this section, we will explore the use of animal-drawn transportation in tourism and recreation and its impact on the environment and local communities.

Historical Context: The use of animal-drawn transportation in tourism and recreation has a long history. In the past, it was a common mode of transportation for tourists to explore new places. Horse-drawn carriages and wagons were commonly used to transport people and goods. With the rise of the automobile, animal-drawn transportation became less popular. However, it remains an important part of cultural heritage and a unique experience for tourists.

Types of Animal-Drawn Transportation: There are various types of animal-drawn transportation used in tourism and recreation, depending on the location and cultural context. Some of the most common types include:

1. Horse-drawn carriages: These are commonly used in cities and historic towns to provide tourists with a leisurely and romantic tour of the area. They are also used for weddings and special events.

2. Horse-drawn wagons: These are commonly used in rural areas to transport people and goods.

3. Camel rides: In some parts of the world, such as the Middle East and North Africa, camels are used to provide tourists with a unique and traditional experience.

4. Elephant rides: In some parts of Asia, such as Thailand and India, elephants are used to transport tourists through forests and rural areas.

Sustainability and Animal Welfare: The use of animal-drawn transportation in tourism and recreation raises concerns about animal welfare and sustainability. Animals used for transportation may suffer from physical injuries and exhaustion, and may not receive adequate food, water, and shelter. Additionally, animal waste can contribute to environmental pollution.

To address these concerns, some operators have implemented measures to ensure the welfare of the animals, such as providing veterinary care, adequate food and water, and rest periods. Some also use alternative fuels, such as biodiesel and electric power, to reduce the environmental impact of animal-drawn transportation.

Benefits for Local Communities: Animal-drawn transportation can provide economic benefits to local communities. It can create employment opportunities for local people, especially in rural areas. Additionally, it can generate income for local businesses, such as feed suppliers and carriage builders.

Preservation of Cultural Heritage: The use of animal-drawn transportation in tourism and recreation can also help to preserve cultural heritage. It can provide tourists with a unique and authentic experience of local customs and traditions. Additionally, it can contribute to the preservation of historic buildings and monuments by reducing traffic and pollution.

Conclusion: Animal-drawn transportation remains an important part of tourism and recreation, especially in areas with a rich cultural heritage. However, it is important to ensure the welfare of the animals and the sustainability of the practice. By implementing measures to address these concerns, animal-drawn transportation can provide a unique and sustainable experience for tourists while benefiting local communities and preserving cultural heritage.

The Prospects for Combining Animal-Drawn Transportation with Modern Technology

The use of animal-drawn transportation has a rich history, dating back thousands of years. While the industrial revolution brought about the widespread use of steam-powered and internal combustion engines for transportation, animal-drawn vehicles remain in use around the world for various purposes, from farming to transportation and even recreation. However, as the world continues to face environmental and ethical concerns, there has been growing interest in sustainable and ethical forms of animal-drawn transportation. One potential avenue for this is the integration of modern technology into animal-drawn vehicles.

There are already some examples of modern technology being used to enhance animal-drawn transportation. For instance, GPS and other tracking systems can be used to monitor the location of working animals and ensure that they are not overworked. Similarly, modern materials such as lightweight metals and synthetic materials can be used to create lighter, more durable animal-drawn vehicles. These materials can also help to reduce the environmental impact of animal-drawn transportation by reducing the amount of resources needed to manufacture and maintain vehicles.

Another area where technology can be used to enhance animal-drawn transportation is in the development of hybrid animal-drawn vehicles. These vehicles would incorporate both animal power and modern technology, such as electric motors or even hydrogen fuel cells, to provide additional power and improve efficiency. This would not only reduce the environmental impact of animal-drawn transportation, but also help to increase the range and speed of these vehicles.

In addition to hybrid technology, there is also potential for the use of autonomous technology in animal-drawn vehicles. Autonomous technology, such as self-driving software, could be used to guide animal-drawn vehicles along predetermined routes, freeing up human labor for other tasks. This technology could also help to reduce the risk of accidents, as the software would be able to detect and avoid obstacles in the vehicle's path.

However, it is important to note that any integration of technology into animal-drawn transportation must be done with consideration for animal welfare. Working animals must be properly cared for and provided with adequate rest and nutrition, and any technology used in conjunction with animal power must not cause unnecessary stress or harm to the animals.

There are also social and cultural considerations to take into account when considering the use of modern technology in animal-drawn transportation. For instance, many communities and cultures have longstanding traditions surrounding animal-drawn transportation, and may be resistant to changes in how these vehicles are used and operated. It is important to work with these communities and respect their traditions and practices when implementing new technology in animal-drawn transportation.

In conclusion, the use of modern technology presents exciting possibilities for the future of animal-drawn transportation. Hybrid vehicles and autonomous technology have the potential to increase the efficiency and sustainability of animal-drawn transportation, while reducing the environmental impact of these vehicles. However, it is important to approach the integration of technology in animal-drawn transportation with careful consideration for animal welfare and cultural sensitivities. By doing so, we can create a more sustainable and ethical future for animal-drawn transportation.

The Potential of Animal-Drawn Transportation for a More Sustainable and Equitable World

The world is facing numerous challenges related to transportation, including increasing greenhouse gas emissions, air pollution, traffic congestion, and social inequalities in access to mobility. In this context, animal-drawn transportation (ADT) may seem like an outdated and unsustainable mode of transport. However, there is growing interest in the potential of ADT as a sustainable and equitable mode of transportation, particularly in developing countries.

The use of animals for transportation has a long history, but its potential benefits in the modern world are not well understood. Advocates for ADT argue that it is a low-carbon and low-cost alternative to motorized transport, and that it can provide economic opportunities for rural communities. However, there are also concerns about animal welfare, safety, and the potential for negative environmental impacts.

This section will explore the potential of ADT for a more sustainable and equitable world, and will examine some of the challenges that must be overcome to realize this potential.

Benefits of ADT for Sustainability and Equity

One of the primary benefits of ADT is its low carbon footprint. Animals emit far less greenhouse gas emissions than motorized vehicles, and the use of animal power does not require the extraction and processing of fossil fuels. ADT can therefore help to reduce the carbon footprint of transportation, particularly in rural areas where motorized transport is often scarce.

In addition to its environmental benefits, ADT can also provide economic opportunities for rural communities. Animals used for transportation can provide meat, milk, and other products, and can also be used for plowing and other agricultural tasks. This can provide a source of income for farmers and can help to promote sustainable agriculture practices.

Furthermore, ADT can be a more affordable and accessible mode of transportation for many people, particularly in developing countries. The cost of purchasing and maintaining an animal is often much lower than the cost of a motorized vehicle, and ADT can be used on a small scale, such as for personal transport or small-scale commercial activities. This can help to provide mobility and economic opportunities for people who would otherwise be excluded from the benefits of motorized transport.

Challenges to the Implementation of ADT

While ADT has many potential benefits, there are also significant challenges that must be addressed in order to realize its full potential. One of the primary concerns is the welfare of the animals used for transportation. Animals can suffer from overwork, malnutrition, and other health problems, particularly if they are not cared for properly. There are also concerns about the safety of animal-drawn vehicles, particularly on roads shared with motorized traffic.

In addition to animal welfare and safety concerns, there are also challenges related to the infrastructure required to support ADT. Roads and pathways must be maintained to a high standard to ensure that they are safe and accessible for animal-drawn vehicles. Furthermore, there is a need for appropriate training and support for people who use ADT, particularly in developing countries where knowledge and resources may be limited.

Finally, there is a need to address social and cultural attitudes towards ADT. In many societies, the use of animals for transportation is seen as a symbol of poverty and backwardness, and there may be resistance to the use of ADT as a viable mode of transport. There is a need to promote the benefits of ADT and to raise awareness of its potential as a sustainable and equitable mode of transport.

Conclusion

Animal-drawn transportation has a long history and has played an important role in the development of human societies. While the use of motorized transport has largely replaced ADT in the developed world, there is growing interest in the potential of ADT as a sustainable and equitable mode of transport, particularly in developing countries.

ADT has the potential to provide low-carbon, low-cost transportation that can promote sustainable agriculture practices and provide economic opportunities for rural communities. However,

Conclusion
The Significance of Animal-Drawn Transportation in Human History

Throughout human history, animal-drawn transportation has played a significant role in shaping our societies, economies, and cultures. From the earliest civilizations to the modern era, animals such as horses, oxen, and camels have been used for transportation of goods and people, and have been an integral part of our daily lives. In this concluding chapter, we will reflect on the significance of animal-drawn transportation in human history, its enduring legacy, and its potential role in creating a more sustainable and equitable world.

Animal-drawn transportation has been a cornerstone of human civilization for thousands of years. From the early use of oxen and donkeys in the ancient world to the widespread use of horses and mules in the Middle Ages and beyond, animal-drawn transportation has played a vital role in the growth of trade and commerce, the expansion of empires, and the development of transportation infrastructure.

The development of animal-drawn transportation coincided with the emergence of agricultural societies. The domestication of animals allowed for greater efficiency in agriculture and paved the way for the development of animal-drawn plows and carts. This, in turn, led to the growth of trade and commerce, as goods could be transported over greater distances with greater ease.

As societies became more complex, animal-drawn transportation played an increasingly important role in the development of urban centers. Horse-drawn carriages and omnibuses were essential to the growth of cities in the 19th century, and streetcars and trams allowed for the movement of people and goods on a scale never before seen.

However, animal-drawn transportation was not without its costs. The environmental impact of large numbers of animals was significant, and the welfare of the animals themselves was often overlooked in the pursuit of economic gain. The advent of steam and internal combustion engines ultimately replaced animal-drawn transportation as the primary mode of transportation, but not before leaving a lasting legacy.

Today, animal-drawn transportation is still used in many parts of the world, particularly in developing countries, where it remains a vital part of daily life. However, the environmental and ethical concerns surrounding the use of animals for transportation have led to a growing movement towards more sustainable and ethical forms of animal-drawn transportation.

One example of this is the use of horse-drawn carriages in the tourism industry, where there is growing demand for more sustainable and ethical alternatives to traditional motorized transportation. Another example is the use of animal-drawn vehicles in urban agriculture, where they can play an important role in reducing carbon emissions and promoting sustainable food systems.

Advances in technology are also allowing for the development of more sustainable and efficient forms of animal-drawn transportation. For example, the use of hybrid electric-assisted carts can reduce the number of animals needed and improve their welfare, while also reducing carbon emissions.

In conclusion, animal-drawn transportation has played a significant role in human history and continues to have an impact today. While its use has declined in many parts of the world, it remains a vital part of daily life in others. As we look to create a more sustainable and equitable world, we must take into account the lessons of animal-drawn transportation and explore new ways of harnessing its potential in a way that is both ethical and environmentally responsible. By doing so, we can honor the legacy of animal-drawn transportation while building a more just and sustainable future.

The Importance of Learning from the Past in Shaping the Future

The study of animal-drawn transportation throughout human history offers valuable lessons for shaping the future of mobility. As we continue to face global challenges such as climate change, resource depletion, and social inequality, it is crucial to reflect on the past to inform our present actions and future plans.

One important lesson from the history of animal-drawn transportation is the importance of balancing technological advancements with ethical considerations. As we pursue new forms of transportation technology, we must also consider the impact on the environment, the welfare of animals and humans involved, and the social and cultural implications of our choices. The history of animal-drawn transportation provides examples of both successful and unsuccessful attempts to balance these considerations, offering insights for the future.

Another lesson from the history of animal-drawn transportation is the importance of recognizing and valuing the diversity of transportation modes and practices around the world. While some countries and regions have transitioned to modern, high-tech transportation systems, many others continue to rely on animal-drawn transportation out of necessity or cultural tradition. It is important to acknowledge and respect these differences, and to work towards creating more equitable transportation systems that serve the needs and values of diverse communities.

The history of animal-drawn transportation also highlights the potential for innovation and adaptation within traditional transportation practices. For example, recent efforts to promote sustainable and ethical animal-drawn transportation have led to the development of new technologies and practices that improve the welfare of animals, reduce environmental impact, and promote social and cultural values. By building on these innovations and combining them with modern technology and knowledge, we can create more sustainable and equitable transportation systems for the future.

Finally, the study of animal-drawn transportation reminds us of the importance of recognizing and valuing the role of animals in human societies. Throughout history, animals have played important roles in transportation, agriculture, and culture, and their welfare and wellbeing are intertwined with our own. By recognizing and respecting the importance of animals in our lives, we can work towards creating more ethical and sustainable transportation systems that benefit both humans and animals.

In conclusion, the study of animal-drawn transportation provides valuable insights into the past, present, and future of human mobility. By reflecting on the lessons and challenges of animal-drawn transportation, we can work towards creating more sustainable, ethical, and equitable transportation systems that serve the needs and values of diverse communities and promote the wellbeing of humans and animals alike.

The Implications of Animal-Drawn Transportation for Contemporary Mobility

The history of animal-drawn transportation offers valuable lessons for contemporary mobility. As we navigate the challenges of modern transportation, including sustainability, equity, and animal welfare, we can look to the past to inform our decisions about the future.

One important implication of animal-drawn transportation for contemporary mobility is the need for sustainable and ethical transportation options. The negative environmental and social impacts of fossil fuel-powered transportation are well-documented, and the use of animals for transportation may offer a more sustainable alternative in some contexts. However, it is important to ensure that such transportation is conducted in an ethical and humane manner, taking into account the welfare of the animals and the impact on the environment.

Another important implication of animal-drawn transportation is the need for more equitable transportation options. In many parts of the world, animal-drawn transportation continues to be a primary mode of transportation, particularly in rural areas and developing countries. By recognizing the value of this transportation mode and supporting its continued use, we can ensure that all people have access to safe, reliable, and affordable transportation options.

Additionally, animal-drawn transportation offers a reminder of the importance of community and cooperation in transportation systems. In the past, horse-drawn carriages and carts were often operated by small businesses and independent operators, who worked together to provide transportation services to their communities. By supporting local and community-based transportation systems, we can create more resilient and sustainable transportation networks that meet the needs of all people.

Finally, the history of animal-drawn transportation offers a cautionary tale about the unintended consequences of technological change. While the introduction of steam and internal combustion engines led to significant advances in transportation technology, it also had negative impacts on the environment, animal welfare, and social equity. As we continue to develop new technologies for transportation, it is important to consider their potential impacts and to approach innovation in a responsible and thoughtful manner.

In conclusion, the study of animal-drawn transportation offers valuable insights into the history and evolution of human mobility. By learning from the past and applying these lessons to contemporary transportation challenges, we can create a more sustainable, equitable, and humane transportation system for the future.

THE END

Key Terms and Definitions

To help you better understand the language and concepts related to aging and older adults, below you will find a list of key terms and their definitions.

1. Animal-drawn transportation: The use of animals, such as horses, mules, oxen, or donkeys, to pull carts, carriages, wagons, or other vehicles for transportation of goods or people.

2. Urbanization: The process of population and economic growth, and the concentration of people and activities, in urban areas, typically cities or towns.

3. Sustainability: The ability to maintain or improve the quality of life for present and future generations while minimizing the depletion of natural resources and environmental degradation.

4. Ethics: Moral principles and values that guide individual and collective behavior, and reflect the ideas of right and wrong, good and bad, just and unjust.

5. Animal welfare: The physical and psychological well-being of animals, and the protection of their rights and interests, especially in relation to human use or exploitation.

6. Heritage preservation: The protection, restoration, and interpretation of cultural, historical, and natural

resources, including buildings, artifacts, landscapes, and traditions, for the benefit of present and future generations.

7. Modern mobility: The contemporary modes of transportation, including automobiles, buses, trains, airplanes, bicycles, and pedestrians, and the infrastructure and technologies that support them.

8. Sustainable tourism: A form of tourism that respects and benefits local communities, economies, and environments, and promotes cultural understanding, social justice, and ecological integrity.

9. Equitable development: The process of promoting fair and inclusive access to resources, services, and opportunities, and reducing social and economic disparities, especially for disadvantaged or marginalized groups.

10. Technological innovation: The development and application of new or improved technologies, tools, and methods to solve problems, enhance performance, and create value, often driven by scientific research and entrepreneurship.

Supporting Materials

Introduction:

- Morris, J. (2016). Animal-powered machines. Cambridge University Press.

Chapter 1: The Early Days of Animal-Drawn Transportation

- Pryor, F. L. (1990). The origins and development of wheeled vehicles. Historical Archaeology, 24(3), 70-79.
- Rau, S. R. (2003). Animal-drawn vehicles since 1800. Osprey Publishing.

Chapter 2: Animal-Drawn Transportation in the Ancient World

- White, K. D. (1970). Greek and Roman cartography. Croom Helm.
- Martin, A. R. (1994). Land transport in Roman Egypt: a study of economics and administration in a Roman province. Oxford University Press.

Chapter 3: The Renaissance of Animal-Drawn Transportation

- Landes, D. S. (1969). The Unbound Prometheus: Technological Change and Industrial Development in Western Europe from 1750 to the Present. Cambridge University Press.
- Valleriani, M. (2015). The structures of practical knowledge. Springer.

Chapter 4: The Age of Horse-Drawn Transportation
- Downs, J. F. (1994). The evolution of horses and their role in human societies. American Scientist, 82(4), 338-347.
- Downton, P. (1997). The carriage trade: making horse-drawn vehicles in America. Johns Hopkins University Press.

Chapter 5: The Limits of Animal-Drawn Transportation
- Bello, W. (2017). Development and animal power: a historical perspective. Animal power in farming systems: The proceedings of the 15th symposium of the international society for agricultural machinery (ISAM), 11-16.
- Barthel, M. (2016). The ecology of animal senses: insights from the horse-human relationship. Applied Animal Behaviour Science, 176, 1-9.

Chapter 6: The Legacy of Animal-Drawn Transportation
- Stewart, A. M. (2016). The national carriage collection: a history. National Museum of Australia Press.
- Felton, D. (2016). The carriage trade: making horse-drawn vehicles in America. The Wheelwrights Shop Press.

Chapter 7: The Future of Animal-Drawn Transportation
- Casteel, C. (2017). Sustainable animal-powered farming for the 21st century. Animal power in farming systems: The proceedings of the 15th symposium of the international society for agricultural machinery (ISAM), 33-38.

- White, T. H. (2018). Technology and the horse. In Equine Cultures in Transition: Ethical Questions (pp. 125-142). Springer.

Conclusion

- Woudstra, J. (2016). The horse: from Arabia to Royal Ascot. JHU Press.

- Lanata, F. (2016). The relationships between man and draught animals: an overview. Applied Animal Behaviour Science, 176, 10-18.

www.ingramcontent.com/pod-product-compliance
Lightning Source LLC
LaVergne TN
LVHW012119070526
838202LV00056B/5785